SATURATED ONCE AND FOR ALL

A Journey in the Life of David

ROB HINES

a people that shall be born, that
he hath done *this*.

his righteousness unto
come, and s...

PSALM 23
A Psalm of David.

THE LORD *is* my shepherd;
I shall not want.
2 He maketh me to lie down
in green pastures: he leadeth
me beside the still . . . he l . . .
3 He restore . . .
leadeth . . .

INTRODUCTION

The denotative meaning of the word *saturated* is to be thoroughly soaked, to take in or soak up energy, liquid, or other substance, to hold as much water or moisture as can be absorbed. In a similar definition, the word ***absorption*** is the process or action by which one thing absorbs or is absorbed by another. The spiritual context of each word is clearly illustrated in scripture through the life of King David.

The anchor text for this understanding occurs first in Samuel and later in 2 Kings

***1 Sam 16**: 1 Now the* Lord *said to Samuel, "How long will you mourn for Saul, seeing I have rejected him from reigning over Israel? Fill your*

horn with oil, and go; I am sending you to Jesse the Bethlehemite. For I have [a]provided Myself a king among his sons." 13 Then Samuel took the horn of oil and anointed him in the midst of his brothers; and the Spirit of the Lord came upon David from that day forward. So Samuel arose and went to Ramah.

The two key points to glean from this passage are: Samuel's horn was filled with oil and God had provided himself a king. It is important to note the Hebrew word for oil is (Shemen) which translated means God's spirit or receiving of God's Spirit.

A similar scene of being anointed for a specific calling comes by way of Jehu in 2 Kings.

__2 Kings 9:1-3__ 9 And Elisha the prophet called one of the sons of the prophets, and said to *him, "Get[a] yourself ready, take this flask of oil in your hand, and go to Ramoth Gilead. ² Now when you arrive at that place, look there for Jehu the son of Jehoshaphat, the son of Nimshi, and go in and make him rise up from among his associates, and take him to an inner room. ³ Then take the flask of oil, and pour it on his head, and say, 'Thus says the LORD: "I have anointed you king over Israel."*

In this passage, the container for God's glory to be poured out is not a horn of oil, as it was in the appointment of David, but rather a flask. To better understand how we perceive God's anointing it is important to understand the function of each vessel. The first vessel, "horn" comes from the Hebrew word "qeren," which means God's strength or power. The second vessel used in the anointing of Jehu was a "flask" which comes from the Hebrew word, "pak." Generally speaking, flasks

are made with human hands from a prestigious material

called alabaster. Symbolically, flask represents human

ingenuity and strength. The parallel with this analysis is

fairly obvious. As believers, we are in a relentless tug-o-

war between our own abilities and God's immutable

strength. Today God's anointing is most often poured out

not from a horn or flask, but from pliable and fleshly

containers: his people. And the effectiveness of this

human vessel, largely comprised of our personal

identities, hinges on two simple questions.

- *How much understanding or ability do we have to carry (absorb) the capacity of God's spirit released in our lives?*

- *How much truth can we hold that will equip us to differentiate between our natural*
strengths and our spiritual strengths?

When we can successfully grapple with answering these two questions, we are one step closer to scratching the surface of understanding God's anointing.

The Anointing. If you have been around church for any length of time, you have probably heard this word in some form (anointed, anoint, anointing). You have likely heard it in a sermon, teaching, or various forms of church lingo, but what is it and what does it mean? The answer is two dimensional.

First, what is it?

To anoint means to smear, rub with oil, typically as a part of a religious ceremony. It was used to ceremonially confirm a divine or holy office upon a priest, prophet, or monarch. In doing so, the chosen one was smeared or rubbed with oil to symbolize an outward identification of an inward spiritual positioning. Typically, this anointing was administered through the pouring of aromatic oil over a person's head or entire body.

Secondly, what does it mean?

The anointing typically means being ordained in terms of an office or purpose for ministry. A varying meaning could also mean to anoint with oil in the context of healing or yoke breaking. A yoke is commonly understood to be a wooden bar or frame by which two animals are joined at the neck to work together on a task. This frame is fitted to a person's shoulders to carry a load in two equal portions, a weight baring structure or burden. Spiritually speaking, the implication of a yoke could be living under an unhappy or difficult state or more specifically, a mindset.

Essentially, the anointing destroys everything that is not of God. It delivers God's people and sets the captives free. In this respect, the anointing is the

presence of God, it's the power of God, and it is the very

person of Jesus. And because the anointing is the person

of Jesus, it, likewise, does what Jesus does- confronts the

spirit of fear in the areas of sickness, depression,

deception, addiction, poverty, and oppression. The

anointing brings deliverance first to the tormented mind

and then to the effect of the symptoms.

The purpose of this book is to focus on David's life

and those who encountered his anointing to better

understand what the anointing is and what it,

emphatically, is not in terms of our own lives.

When it comes to the modern-day church, there

is a pervasive belief that the anointing is needed for

everything. This is a widely held, but false, belief without a determinable basis of fact or natural explanation. It's simply untrue. We don't need the anointing. We are in the anointing already, every single day because we are in Christ and he is in us, but what is it that causes us to accept the notion of needing the anointing anew each day? David was anointed, saturated if you will, only once, *once and for all.*

His bad deeds did not disqualify him from God's anointing nor did his good deeds make him more saturated in it. He was as saturated as he was ever going to be from the moment he was selected, from the very moment of conception- the moment his spiritual life began. The same could be said of us as believers. We are chosen, appointed, and called, and that is enough. Yet, we often believe otherwise. Why?

Is our need for a perpetual renewal of the anointing a Biblical belief or is it merely a deeply held, tradition rooted in religiosity? According to *Mark 7:13*

They made the word of God of no effect through your

tradition which you have handed down. And many such

things you do." As believers, it is time we cast aside our

man-made traditions and cling to the truth of His word.

Contents

—

VNXIT · TE · DOMINVS · SVPER · HÆREDITATEM

Chapter 1

Connected to God

Our journey through David's life clearly illustrates how the anointing was a complete work from the beginning but develops in the life of David as he allows the absorption of the holy spirit to fulfill his purpose and destiny. The same principle can be applied to us as believers. Yes, we are as anointed as we will ever be the day Christ chooses and calls us, but as with David, an absorption process of that anointing must occur before we can become the spiritual champions that God has called us to be.

Everyone has a starting point. For David, his anointing started with a connection to God that beckons each of us to consider the same questions David asked himself. Am I connected to God, and is God connected to me?

From a young age, David clearly understood that he was connected to God, but sadly, this connection alienated him from his earthly father and his brothers. As a result, his early life was riddled with rejection and bitterness. David starts his battle of rejection from a natural stance. He is left out of the party as the prophet Samuel comes to anoint a king from the house of Jesse. Perhaps David's father, Jesse, erroneously believed Samuel's declaration that "a king would be found in his household" would stop with his first son, Eliab, the son he favored most. When Eliab was rejected, Jesse called for all seven brothers to pass before the prophet before he finally admitted that there was, indeed, another brother, an unworthy brother, David, in the field tending the sheep. As David arrived, Samuel heard the word of the

Lord, "Rise and anoint him; this is the one." (v12) The scene of the envious brothers seething with anger as Samuel takes the horn of oil and anoints young David in the presence of his enemies is not difficult to imagine. Undoubtedly in that moment, his brothers fertilized a root of bitterness that began to grow and serve as David's first challenge.

To fulfill his calling, David had to overcome rejection and address the root of bitterness in his life to receive true healing through the anointing that breaks the yoke. Rejection, as it relates to medicine, means an immunological response that refuses to accept substances or organisms that are recognized as foreign. As the prophet Samuel releases the order of God in David's life, his brothers come to further identify David as a foreign object in their household, and he likewise, refuses to accept the substance of their negativity, understanding their rejection will distract him from his higher calling. In this respect, David's first spiritual attack of the enemy is an attempt to strike a deep familial wound that threatens to drive a wedge in David's ability to trust God if he does not fight this temptation with the sword of the word. Through the saturation of the word, David comes to realize connection means joining through communication and his first allegiance is a connection to his heavenly father, even if it means forsaking his earthly father and his jealous brothers. Yet, his family's refusal to accept, submit, or even believe David would become King (as promised in this scene) renders David with a feeling of unworthiness that he mostly likely battles him his entire life.

The same could be said of Christians who have been anointed and selected by God for a divine purpose, which is really to say all of us. We will, likewise, battle insecurities of unworthiness, but it is our connection to God that will propel us to understand what it truly means to be anointed. In moments of doubt, we must cling to the truth of God's word and allow David's story to serve as a reminder that God's ways are not our ways, and his thoughts are not our thoughts. (Isaiah 55:8) V 12 David did not look the part, nor do we at times, but God was not submitting to the whims of Israel and pandering to their image of what a king should look like. The order of God was choosing a King for himself, which is precisely why Samuel was charged to arise and anoint him. His rising was a sign of honor and recognition to the King who was being established. As Samuel takes the horn and literally pours (saturates) David's head with oil he is, more importantly, saturating David with the word and with God himself, which cannot be undone. As evidenced throughout scripture time and time again, what God anoints cannot be reversed.

It is important to note that God literally begins David's life with a physical and spiritual saturation of his anointing to serve as a reminder of who he is connected to, but he does not stop there. He also connects him to a leader who becomes influential in his purpose, a purpose that ultimately prepares David's heart and mind to understand God is not merely anointing him with oil but rather covering him with his power and presence in order to protect him from every area the enemy would use to strike or expose as weakness.

Chapter 2

Connected to a Leader

I Samuel 16:14- 23

[14] But the Spirit of the LORD departed from Saul, and a distressing spirit from the LORD troubled him. [15] And Saul's servants said to him, "Surely, a distressing spirit from God is troubling you. [16] Let our master now command your servants, *who are* before you, to seek out a man *who is* a skillful player on the harp. And it shall be that he will play it with his hand when the [a]distressing spirit from God is upon you, and you shall be well." [17] So Saul said to his servants, [b]"Provide me now a man who can play well, and bring *him* to me."[18] Then one of the servants answered and said, "Look, I

have seen a son of Jesse the Bethlehemite, *who is* skillful in playing, a mighty man of valor, a man of war, prudent in speech, and a handsome person; and the Lord *is* with him." ¹⁹ Therefore Saul sent messengers to Jesse, and said, "Send me your son David, who *is* with the sheep." ²⁰ And Jesse took a donkey *loaded with* bread, a skin of wine, and a young goat, and sent *them* by his son David to Saul. ²¹ So David came to Saul and stood before him. And he loved him greatly, and he became his armorbearer. ²² Then Saul sent to Jesse, saying, "Please let David stand before me, for he has found favor in my sight." ²³ And so it was, whenever the spirit from God was upon Saul, that David would take a harp and play *it* with his hand. Then Saul would become refreshed and well, and the distressing spirit would depart from him.

David's connection to a leader, which eventually spurs him in his purpose was not by accident. In God, there is a requirement for spiritual maturity that evolves through a process. God is a God of order who demands we hold fast to the process, which is exactly happens with David. He does not move from the pasture to the palace overnight. However, it is the quiet and solitary moment of worship in the pasture that sets him up for opportunity when King Saul desperately needs the melodic hum of a harp to soothe him from his torment. In this respect, David finds his way to the palace from the purity of his worship when nobody was watching. Without question, he was a skillful player who had perfected his craft through obedience day in and day out, but more importantly, he was an anointed worshipper whose hidden gem (gift) was connecting the position of his heart to a holy God who would catapult his calling and purpose into action by causing others around him to take notice of his talents and anointing.

Truly, he was playing in faithful obedience for an audience of "One," but in doing so, through divine providence, others began to take note, particularly the servant of Saul who vouches for David by describing him as a handsome man, a skillful musician, a mighty man of valor, prudent of speech, and a man of war. It is important to note that David's end goal was never to secure favor with King Saul, as he never even knew King Saul's servant was watching him closely. His appointment in the court was only a byproduct of his desire to use every available training to hone his gift and merely praise and love the true King through song. Yet, through his willingness to offer his gifts to God in worship, he received God's approval in the form of the servant's attention. As a result, King Saul could not refuse the servant's stellar recommendation of David.

The same can be said of believers who use their talents to glorify God. In fact, one of the most tangible ways to identify God's anointing on a person's life is in direct proportion to the way others begin to identify Godly character, even when it is still underdeveloped. However, as with David, these gifts do not stay underdeveloped.

As David enters the king's court, his skills and confidence begin to develop even more, so much so that King Saul is impressed enough to appoint David as his armor bearer, one of the highest positions in the royal court. In addition, he tells Jesse that David has found favor in his sight. He even becomes a spiritual advisor to King Saul. In doing so, he enters a learning stage where he begins to establish his own philosophies regarding how he will govern God's people when it is his time to be king. This learning stage starts with the realization that he does not want to lead in the same manner of Saul who is constantly leading through a self-preservation mindset. David begins to understand that King Saul was selected through the love of people, which, in turn, causes him to live in a constant state of emotional turmoil where his chief desire is to please people and placate their emotions more than God. In these observations, David purposes in his heart to lead in a different manner, one that seeks only to please God. Naturally, this becomes the downfall of Saul's jealousy toward David, the same jealousy David experienced as a young boy with his own father and brothers. This jealousy ushers in division between Saul and David that eventually paves the way for David to be king.

Undoubtedly, losing fellowship with Saul, who became a father-like figure to David, was a painful reminder of the rejection he encountered as a young boy, but like with the animosity of his father and brothers, David is keenly aware that not every stage in the maturation process of God's will is pleasurable. In fact, some of the most difficult stages are actually the greatest opportunities for growth, growth that occurred because he was in the right place (the palace) and connected to a leader he could truly learn from, even if it was often a difficult road that, more times than not, taught him more about how he did not want to lead.

Amid Saul's failing ministry and false security that his kingship was still intact, God faithfully sends David a different kind of leader for encouragement. Jonathan, the son of Saul, becomes David's closest confidant and teaches him about authentic brotherhood. 1 Samuel 18:1

describes their bond as one whose souls were knitted together, which according to Deuteronomy 13:6 is like a friend who is as your own soul, meaning one who is a companion of one's innermost thoughts and feelings. This bond is described again in Proverbs 18:24 as a friend who sticks closer than a brother. Jonathan is the kind of friend who could be trusted with the most vulnerable places of David's heart and speaks truth to him without risk of offense. The friendship between Jonathan and David becomes so intertwined Jonathan humbly bestows his royal robe, armor, and even his sword, bow, and belt on David as if to say, "Where you go, I go with you." This humble act of service in the natural mirrors the spiritual covenant God has with David when he promises the same, "Wherever you go, I go with you."

Clinging to God's covenant and cloaked in His righteousness, David is fully connected to his heavenly father and understands his connection to two different types of earthly leaders (both Saul and Jonathan) serves as a steppingstone for his eternal purpose.

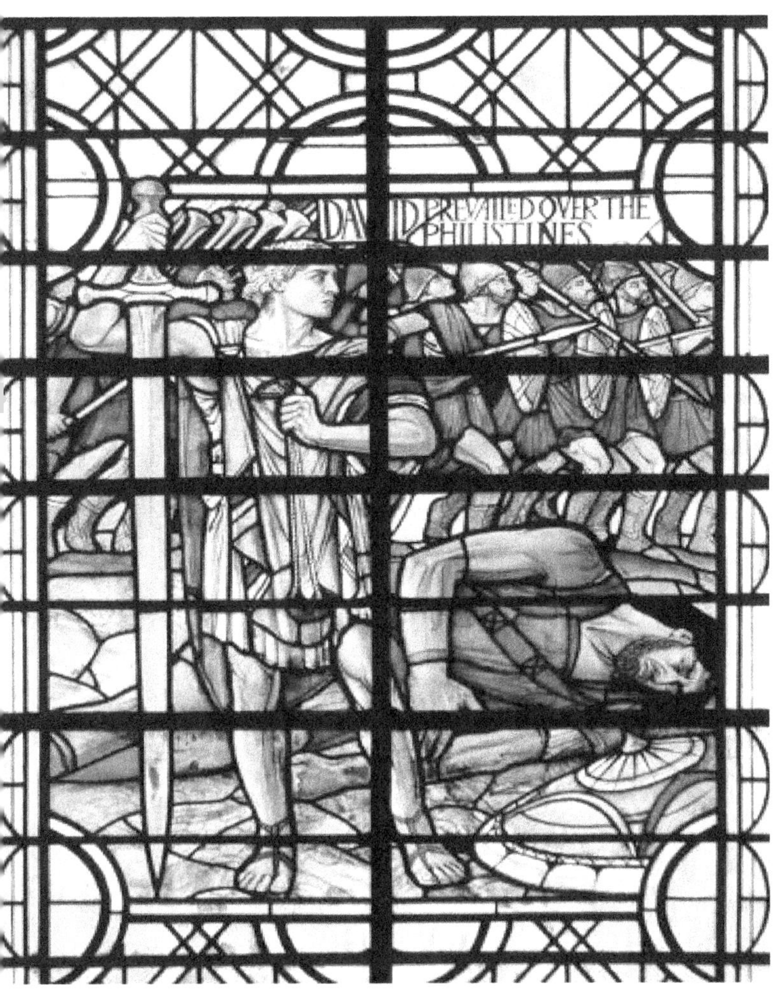
DAVID PREVAILED OVER THE
PHILISTINES

Chapter 3
Connected to Purpose

In considering the promise of his purpose to become the king of Israel, David undoubtedly experiences confusion over why he has suddenly become the object of Saul's hatred. He made it to the palace for what would seem to be the training ground for kingship. He entertained Saul with his harp, counseled him, and even defeated Goliath. Yet, the striking blow to Saul's pride when the people boasted, "Saul has slain his thousands, but David his tens of thousands" proves to be more than Saul can handle, so he pursues David on foot for the soul purpose of killing him. Coincidentally, had it not been for Jonathan's honorable and loving loyalty to David in warning him of impending destruction, then aiding him to the point of putting his own life in jeopardy, David never would have found safety or protection in the cave of Adullam. As David retreats in the cave of confusion and weariness, he, most likely, entertains the thought that this is not the blessed and anointed life he had envisioned.

His confusion proves that even when anointed for a specific purpose, life does not always line up with our perceptions of what blessed looks like. Yet, it is most often in the cave (not the palace) where the demand of the anointing provides the greatest abilities. It is in this wilderness experience where David begins to trust and lean on God beyond what he already knows. More specifically, the cave forces David, and us, to trust resources that can only be found in a relationship of God's spirit.

While he is grappling with his own emotional insecurity, many men begin to follow him into the wilderness to escape their own persecution. As such,

"Adullam" becomes a caved fortress, a stronghold for the

tired and destitute, a place of refuge where they can bring

their own problems, but at that point, David was not

interested in helping others with their problems. He was

looking for a reprieve from his own trauma.

In all, 400 men gathered with David, and they

weren't there to offer David help. Quite the contrary,

they were seeking help for themselves. Surely, David

must have thought, "God, why these men? These men

are distressed, broke, and discontented. I have enough

problems of my own. I need strong and wealthy men to

help me out of this crisis." Yet, David was shortsighted in

his understanding that a cave was never designed to keep

a man of God but rather to advance him. Adullam means

"Justice of the People," and justice is exactly what the

men who declared David their leader received. They

became justified from debt and despair and embraced an identity in God, which is to say that of a champion. Through aiding these societal outcasts, David quickly learns that in the wilderness the anointing will not only sustain him, but it will also break the yoke of weariness, fatigue and impart longsuffering to him.

Without a doubt, the release of leadership with this small group was necessary for the manifestation of God's spirit in positioning David for his future of leading a nation. In leading others, David comes to realize the restoration of his own healing comes through helping others. Proving himself to be trustworthy in leading, even from a place of personal despair, God sees that David can be trusted with more, so he sends the prophet Gad to urge David to depart Adullam by saying, "Do not stay in this stronghold. Go to the land of Judah." 1 Samuel 22:5

Gad's obedient word to move from this stronghold reminds David that the weight of being trapped in one place under the pressure of others' heaviness cannot stop the movement of God's purpose. On the contrary, the adversity actually strengthens the purpose and reminds believers of a core truth, the same truth the Apostle Paul preached to the church of Philippi when he said, "I can do all things through Christ (anointing) who strengthens me." Phil. 4:13

The prophet Gad's name literally means a chisel, a pointed iron or steel bar for loosening ore or rock. By using the prophet Gad to steer David, God is, in essence, chipping away at the shallow places of David's carnal thinking to produce a pliable heart that will allow him to move beyond what he can see or feel and into a place where he can lead in truth, integrity, and Godly character. In this respect, God knows David's heart better than David knows himself. He knows the mental fatigue and physical anguish from the cave experience where others were looking to David for answers, coupled with David's personality, is cultivating the anointing, and drawing out necessary gifts for leadership that will serve him well later. However, this refinement process is not only for David's benefit. When the spirt of the Lord's purpose is being released in the Earth, it is not just for one individual, but for all. This is evident in the fact that the power of the anointing is, indeed, transforming David's life, but more importantly, it is transforming the lives of those who have united with him. These men, who were previously wrought in debt and despair, are now champions of the faith fully equipped for service due, in large part, to David's leadership. As a leader, David does not allow these men to stay in the same conditions in which he found them. Through the anointing, his spiritual influence causes these previously oppressed men to understand the freedom that awaits those who serve others in Christ.

During David's time in the king's court, he was connected to the leadership of Saul where he vowed to lead in a different manner when he became king of Israel, but what he didn't realize at the time was the bridge to the throne is always paved with stones of adversity. As such, his ascension to the throne required a testing of his leadership abilities with a small group of men in a cold and lonely cave in order to prepare him for his purpose, which was to serve the whole nation of Israel as king.

Chapter 4

Connected to Service

"If you serve the purpose, the purpose will serve you." -

Pastor Rob Hines

To serve means to perform duties or services for
another person or organization, or to be of use in
achieving or satisfying a purpose. After his time in the
cave of Adullum, David understands service better than
most. He comes to fully understand the release of serving
the anointing, and through his actions, aligns his service
to the definition outlined in I Peter 4:11. "Whoever
serves (let it be) as one who serves by the strength that
God supplies in order that in everything God may be
glorified through Jesus Christ." Through adversity, David
has reached a place where his chief goal is the same

pledge he made in the king's court: to be a man after

God's own heart. He listens to the heart of God,

demonstrates a life committed to surrendering to the

purpose of the anointing, and leads those around him

how to do the same. He exemplifies the kingdom

principle that learning to lead is synonymous with

learning to serve beyond yourself, and one of the best

ways he serves is through his actions in being pursued by

Saul.

As Saul is in hot pursuit of David with the intent of

killing him, Saul unknowingly stops to rest in the very cave

where David and his men are hiding. In this moment,

David and his men have every opportunity to seize Saul

and cause him great harm, but it is in this moment that

David does something altogether different. Rather than

capitalizing on the opportunity for revenge to the point of

death, he exemplifies a deeper absorption of the

anointing. In this passage of scripture, we clearly see how the principle of learning through serving and maturing causes an individual to be transformed through the purpose of life and the power of the kingdom.

1 Samuel 24:1-7

^{1}After Saul returned from pursuing the Philistines, he was told, "David is in the Desert of En Gedi." ^{2}So Saul took three thousand able young men from all Israel and set out to look for David and his men near the Crags of the Wild Goats. ^{3}He came to the sheep pens along the way; a cave was there, and Saul went in to relieve himself. David and his men were far back in the cave. ^{4}The men said, "This is the day the LORD spoke of when he said to you, 'I will give your enemy into your hands for you to deal with as you wish.'" Then David crept up unnoticed and cut off a corner of Saul's robe. ^{5}Afterward, David was conscience-stricken for having cut off a corner of his robe. ^{6}He said to his men, "The LORD forbid that I should do such a thing to my master, the LORD's anointed, or lay my hand on him; for he is the anointed of the LORD." ^{7}With these words David sharply rebuked his men and did not allow them to attack Saul. And Saul left the cave and went his way.

In this scene, King Saul puts himself in a situation

that leaves him defenseless as he is completely unaware

that David and his men are in the recesses of the cave.

Here, David has a perfect opportunity to end the saga of

events with King Saul. In addition, he is being enticed by his mighty men with a tempting plea, "God is putting your enemy in your hands to do as you wish." David momentarily heeds to the temptation, even to the point of cutting the corner of Saul's robe— a sign that he could have easily killed Saul. Yet, in a defining moment, David ceases the final act of murder and instead, hearkens to the voice of God over the popularity of the people, which was the very battle Saul could never win. Before these men, he even audibly repents for tearing the garment and vows not to lay a hand on the anointed. The picture here is one of David's obedience to lead from his spiritual heart, rather than from his head full of carnal knowledge.

In doing so, he is modeling the ultimate act of service to the mighty men who are watching and seeking to emulate him. In this respect, David is providing on the job training for these men and doesn't even know it. He is allowing his men to see what a life consecrated to God looks like and is simultaneously equipping them with a higher level of spiritual awareness. David's words serve as a warning that even though he may have had personal rights and the human approval that killing Saul was the right thing to do, neither of these justifications trumped God's approval. In essence, David is giving them a glimpse of what it means to have a deeper spiritual understanding and is teaching them that even in the midst of pressure from natural events, a Godly person has a responsibility to exercise restraint and be sensitive to the discernment of what the Holy Spirit desires to do.

It is also important to note that David's act of cutting Saul's robe not only indicates that he could have killed Saul, it also indicates that David has touched the position of where the anointing resides. Biblical interpretation suggests the train of a robe was an indication of a king's power. The robe also symbolizes the amount of territory a king has conquered or the territory which belongs to him, as evidenced by the description in Isaiah 6:1 that says, "I saw the Lord (King of Kings) sitting on the throne, and the train of his robe filled the temple." God's robe is the longest train to ever fill the earth. His rule and reign are supreme, yet he has given men in the earth the same authority. Saul was one such man.

Though the Bible does not give a definitive description of the size of Saul's robe, it is safe to assume it was rather large as God had placed him as king over Israel and allowed him to rule over all God's people and his territory. David understands this, which is why he flees from the temptation to murder God's anointed. Yet, with the cutting of Saul's robe a marked transition of power begins to take place. Saul's reign is coming to an end. Shortly, after this incident, Saul becomes so tormented that he asks his servant to kill him. Saul's self-inflicted

death, ushers in the dawning of a new and triumphant

King David who is ready, willing, and able to serve God

with his whole heart and establish a clear vision for the

people of Israel.

Chapter 5

Connected to the Vision

David's life was shaped by the events leading up to his reign as king of Israel. His time humbly tending sheep in the field, faithfully playing his harp in the king's court, miraculously defeating Goliath, desperately fleeing from Saul, and courageously hiding in the Cave of Adullam were all instrumental in preparing him to successfully fulfill his destiny, which was to become king at a very young thirty years old. In all, David reigned as king for forty years. In Hebron, he reigned over Judah for seven years, and in Jerusalem, he ruled over all Israel for thirty three years.

Like much of his formative years, David's regime as king was marked by periods of highs and lows. He found favor in God's sight and enjoyed a period of prosperity, but he also committed adultery, plotted the murder of Uriah, and mourned the death of his son, proving once again that his anointing was not contingent upon his actions but rather God's sovereignty. However, oddly enough, David's time on the throne is not nearly as important as his ascent and descent from the throne. The same could be said of us in that where we are going is not nearly as vital as the God-ordained process by which we arrived at the position God has called us to, or how we leave it.

Despite any missteps in his long life, the same oil that was poured from Samuel's horn onto the head of a ruddy 15-year-old David, the young overlooked shepherd boy was still present in the grey hairs of a dying 70-year-old, decorated and distinguished, King David. The anointing of God never left David's life. David did not need to ask for a fresh anointing with each new battle he faced. He was as anointed as he was ever going to be the minute he was connected to a holy God through the symbolic pouring out of oil. The only variable that changed in the fifty-year period was David's awareness of the degree to which he had absorbed God's blessed anointing. By the end of David's life, it is evident that he fully understands the purpose for his time on earth. The purpose of his life was to serve, but the purpose of his death was to establish a vision. This is evident through David's final words and his final request.

The 23rd chapter of 2 Samuel begins with the final words of David and illuminates the character of his followers in that they are now not only serving David but serving a vision greater than all of them combined. Some of the same individuals who came to David in distress at the cave of Adullam are now identified as "David's Mighty

Men." This is truly the power of the anointing's

transformative ability in our individual lives. Simply put,

the anointing transforms people's lives from ordinary to

supernatural and is released within groups of believers for

the agenda of advancing the kingdom of God's purpose

and ultimate dominion. The key details of these two

verses serve as a summation of David's life and illustrate

an important roadmap for the anointing.

> **23** Now these *are* the last words of David.
> *Thus* says David the son of Jesse;
> *Thus* says the man raised up on high,
> The anointed of the God of Jacob,
> And the sweet psalmist of Israel:
> ² "The Spirit of the LORD spoke through me,
> And His word *was* on my tongue.

a) David was the son of Jesse- each of us has a beginning

point. (Connected to God)

b) He was the man raised up on high- each of us has a

repositioning in life (Connected to a Leader)

c) He was anointed of God- each of us obtains strength

from the Lord (Connected to Purpose)

d) He spoke the spirit of the Lord- each of us must yield

to God's purpose (Connected to Service)

e) His word was on David's tongue- each of us must

release the Word in the Earth (Connected to Vision)

Clearly, David's purpose was to serve, and he

always served by connecting people to the vision of God

by having God's word on his tongue. This same word,

which provides a glimpse of the omnipotent an

omnipresent nature of God, was prophesied by Isaiah

(46:10) when he declared, "God's counsel will stand." In

other words, God's vision will always be established

regardless of who sits on an earthly throne. This is

because God has no origin. "I am that I am" implies the

self-existence of God.

Origin is a word that is only applicable to created things. When we consider anything with an origin, we are not thinking of God, as God is self-existent. He was not created by a thing but rather was the creator of all things, or as A.W. Tozer phrases it, "Aside from God, nothing is self-caused."

As with David, and with us, God creates purpose for our lives and because he is not confined to time, he sees our life's purpose as a whole. It is, he, and he, alone, who could see the end from the beginning, just as he did with David. Through the anointing made manifest in the form of wisdom, David is able to grasp the finality of his life as it compares to the infinite reach of God's sovereignty, and it is this wisdom that, bids him to request a cup of water on his death bed. With this seemingly carnal request in 2 Samuel 23:15-16, David is activating the initial stage of the anointing "Changing Hands."

In the same way that the mantle of the anointing was passed from Saul to David, David is transferring the anointing to those that will come after him. The mighty men described in this chapter are experiencing the end to what was once, a familiar place in their lives, and just as with David, and each of us, everyone must start somewhere. These men embraced change, which requires the understanding that an end must come before a new purpose can begin. An analysis of David's final request for "A Cup of Water," sets the stage for three important transitions of the anointing.

I Samuel 23 13 During harvest time, three of the thirty chief warriors came down to David at the cave of Adullam, while a band of Philistines was encamped in the Valley of Rephaim. 14 At that time David was in the stronghold, and the Philistine garrison was at Bethlehem. 15 David longed for water and said, "Oh, that someone would get me a drink of water from the well near the gate of Bethlehem!" 16 So the three mighty warriors broke through the Philistine lines, drew water from the well near the gate of Bethlehem and carried it back to David. But he refused to drink it; instead, he poured it out before the Lord. 17 "Far be it from me, Lord, to do this!" he said. "Is it not the blood of men who went at the risk of their lives?" And David would not drink it.

The first transition of the anointing is in the natural. David has a longing for the water from the wells of Bethlehem, meaning house of bread. He is thirsty, but he needs a very specific water. Matthew 5:6 describes it as, "Blessed are those who hunger and thirst for righteousness, for they shall be filled." Spiritually and symbolically, David longs for a filling of God's spirit in his heart. In this appeal, he is sending a direct message to his followers. According to God's word, thirsty is contagious, and his men begin to take notice. Through this request, they, and all believers that were to come after David—which is to say all of us—begin to see that nothing will satisfy us like the righteousness of God.

The life of David now demands others respond to the saturation time they have spent with him, and in doing so, a distinct transition is taking place. The purpose of David's anointing was to serve God's people, and the anointing is now transitioning to the purpose of others sustaining the vision.

The second transition of the anointing is in the form of obedience to serve while acknowledging service is often merely trusting God to accomplish the impossible. Specifically, verse 16 says, "Three of the mighty men heard the words of David and without thought served the word spoken." Though likely frightened, these three men courageously broke through a garrison, which is defined as a permanent military installation, to secure the water David was craving. They literally put their lives at stake for a cup of water. Keep in mind, they could have gotten water anywhere nearby and called it water of Bethlehem, but often it is not "the easy" that makes it God's purpose. After all, if you can do it on your own, is it even God's purpose? So, the question then becomes, why? Why did these men go to such desperate and dangerous lengths to obtain a seemingly insignificant cup of water? The answer is quite simple. They heard a word from their leader, they positioned and accepted the word in their hearts, and believed God was using David as his mouthpiece. Therefore, if David said it, God must have had a purpose in it. It is important to note that there is never an indication of the men questioning, "Should we really do this?" They simply took it upon themselves to serve the need. Without a doubt, God still desires the same faithful, unwavering obedience from his followers.

The final transition of the anointing is in the form of surrender. In verse 16, the men carried the water back to David. These three men complete their mission by offering David the cup of water, a cup of water that was only secured after the word "go" was released in their hearts by God's servant. In this climactic scene, David wraps his feeble fingers around the cup of what started out as a thirst, was then released through his spirit as a word, and is finally received as the fulfillment of God's promise iterated in Matthew 5:6 with the declaration that, "Hunger and thirst shall be filled."

In this defining moment, David does something so interesting. He now holds the coveted promise which will fulfill the desperation of his physical need, but rather than putting the cup to his parched lips, he gently tilts the cup to the ground and pours out every glorious drop. As he pours the sacrificial water on the ground, the act could have, at first, been viewed as a sign of ingratitude to the men who sacrificed so much to obtain it, but the truth was quite the opposite. The pouring of the water serves as a spiritual symbol that David is pouring out the sweet cup of God's mercy so his anointing can permeate the earth for generations to come.

It is important to note, this scene of David refusing the satisfying water from Bethlehem serves as a direct contrast to the future bitter cup Christ requests to pass from him. When Christ, the son of David, born in Bethlehem (the vey place where David's valiant men retrieve the water) willingly drinks from the bitter, metaphorical cup of death, he finishes the job of David's anointing once and for all. Both men literally died pouring out their lives for the hope of humanity. In this respect, the transition of the anointing always comes by way of surrender.

David is willing to surrender because he knows the cup is a vessel for holding liquid/ water, and water is a symbol of God's promise of his spirit fulfilling the word. If

David drinks the cup, it symbolizes that he is the only vessel who has the ability to carry God's anointing, but instead, by pouring the water out unto the Lord, the act signifies that the same anointing that was with David is now transcending in the men's lives through this act of bravery and servanthood. David also knows his life has been so blessed with God's anointing that it is his obligation and privilege to release God's anointing into the earth for those who are going to continue after him. In essence, David is releasing the anointing back where it came from and making the Lord's spirit available for all eternity, transcending from generation to generation and fulfilling the prophecy that David's position of kingship would be established throughout the earth, not just in the physical nature of the kingdom but also the spiritual.

David's act of surrender with the cup of water also seals God's covenant with David as promised in 2 Samuel 7:10-

17 when God declares, "He shall build a house for my name, and I will establish the throne of his Kingdom forever." That kingdom, the house that David built, still stands today and serves as an example for all in how serving God, while being supplied with the anointing of his spirit, is an everlasting fulfillment of utter joy that has the potential of turning even a rank sinner into a champion of the faith.

work
attitude
commitment
focus ability
Champion
courage
practice
dedication

Final Remarks

Before the opening of the 2021 MLB Season, Kevin Costner was interviewed about the movie, *Field of Dreams*, a 30-year-old production. When asked his thoughts regarding the building of the "new" major league field that was constructed on the site of the film's original set, Kevin Costner said, ""When you set out to build anything you want to overdevelop it." This statement correlates to the way God built David's anointing and how he builds ours as well.

God, through his anointing, has provided "an overdeveloped ability" to every person who submits to his calling and purpose. He has also supplied every resource necessary for a life of service to the King.

The totality of David's life serves as a reminder that the anointing of God, "The Cup" will continually be chiseled and redefined in our lives, but the full capacity of God's spirit within the cup was released to all of us from the beginning when he promised to create a field of champions out of all of us.

In the movie, *The Field of Dreams,* the iconic quote, "If you build it, they will come" has become quite memorable for most Americans. However, in the spiritual sense, God has already built "it"- meaning the anointing, and he has graciously released it to those who are willing to face the field of life as champions in his anointing. Far too often, we are confused about God's anointing. The spirit of God was never intended to be a little dab of do every time life throws you a curve ball. God has released the full saturation of his presence in, and over, your life so that in serving him you will have the ability to show others that there is something Greater in you (and your life) that can only be explained by your devotion to a life of serving God.

Now the charge is this. Will you be the one who allows God's spirit to set an example for others,

so they understand they can have the same encounter?
Will it be easy? Absolutely not.

Ziklag is the place of one of David's greatest curve
balls. In 1 Samuel 30: 1-8 David provides

readers a glimpse of one of his greatest challenges in
remembering where his help comes from.

30 David and his men reached Ziklag on the third
day. Now the Amalekites had raided the Negev and Ziklag.
They had attacked Ziklag and burned it, ² and had taken
captive the women and everyone else in it, both young
and old. They killed none of them, but carried them off as
they went on their way.³ When David and his men
reached Ziklag, they found it destroyed by fire and their
wives and sons and daughters taken captive. ⁴ So David
and his men wept aloud until they had no strength left to
weep. ⁵ David's two wives had been captured—Ahinoam
of Jezreel and Abigail, the widow of Nabal of
Carmel. ⁶ David was greatly distressed because the men
were talking of stoning him; each one was bitter in spirit
because of his sons and daughters. But David found
strength in the LORD his God.⁷ Then David said to
Abiathar the priest, the son of Ahimelek, "Bring me the
ephod." Abiathar brought it to him, ⁸ and David
inquired of the LORD, "Shall I pursue this raiding party?
Will I overtake them?""Pursue them," he answered. "You
will certainly overtake them and succeed in the rescue."

After the overwhelming news of all being lost or as one might say, "things closest to home being gone," David's "Champion Men" who have matured so much in their faith, now want to stone David over their personal losses. Yet, David never loses the focus of the place in his heart of God's anointing. He knows exactly where his strength comes from, which is why he takes the ephod and inquires of the Lord. The Lord releases the word that carries the anointing when he tells David to pursue, overtake, and recover all.

- David's challenging test to, once again seek God's counsel over man's, reminds each of us as believers that there will be times when we must stand, what seems to be, completely alone. However, when

God brings us to this, often lonely, field to be a champion, he never leaves us alone. He stands with us and always gets the final say as stated in Revelation 12:10. "Then I heard a loud voice saying in Heaven, now salvation and strength and the kingdom of God, and the power of his Christ (anointed one) have come, for the accuser of our brethren, who accused them before our God day and night has been cast down."

When we are operating in God's anointing, we are never truly forsaken, even when we feel abandoned. As such we can always find God, in the same place he found us: surrender. In surrender, he becomes our fierce advocate and fights our battles for us, just as he did for 19-year old David when he granted him the strength to topple a massive giant.

Yet, this sacred anointing begs a few questions.

Are you connected to God?

Are you connected to a leader?

Are you connected to purpose?

Are you connected to service?

Are you connected to the vision?

More specifically, can you see the end from the beginning, and is the saturation of God's presence being absorbed in your life the way it was for David? When it came to the saturation of God's presence through the anointing, a vessel was always used to dispense his glory. The journey of David's life shows us that Samuel used the horn of oil to pour out the anointing on David. Similarly, David used the cup of water to pour out the anointing on his mighty followers, and finally, Christ used the vessel of his body to pour out the blood anointing on each of us under the new covenant. Knowing we are justified by Christ's blood, baptized in water, and anointed with His oil to serve a role in an eternal vision gives us no time to waste.

"It's time to arise and come to the field of champions yourself. It's time to remember you are a champion in a field of champions because you are, first, connected to God's original purpose."

- Pastor Rob Hines

Notes

1. MERRIAM-WEBSTER'S COLLEGIATE DICTIONARY, 11th ed., Merriam-Webster, 2003.

2. Tozer, A.W. *The Knowledge of the Holy* (Milton, Keyenes United Kingdom: Authentic Media, 2005).

3. Hines, Robert. Collected Sermons.

4. Robinson, and W P. Kinsella. *Field of Dreams*. Universal City, CA: Universal, 1999.